Music Minus One

3413A

Oboe Classics

for the

Advanced Player

Stanislas Verroust

Solos de Concert

Piano Accompaniments

3413A

Oboe Classics

for the

Advanced Player

✦✦✦

PIANO ACCOMPANIMENTS

✦✦✦

ISBN 1-59615-360-1

2eme Solo de Concert
for Oboe & Piano

Stanislas Verroust, op. 74

Mosso moderato

a son Elève Fernand Magnien

3ᵐᵉ Solo de Concert

Stanislas Verroust, op. 74

Moderato

21

MMO 3413A

Engraving: Wieslaw Novak

MMO 3413A

MUSIC MINUS ONE
50 Executive Boulevard
Elmsford, New York 10523-1325
800.669.7464 U.S. — 914.592.1188 International

www.musicminusone.com
info@musicminusone.com